EPHESIANS

SCRIPTURE STUDY NOTEBOOK

NASB SCRIPTURE STUDY NOTEBOOK: EPHESIANS
Copyright © 2022 by Three Sixteen Publishing Inc.
Steadfast Bibles is a division of Three Sixteen Publishing Inc.
Requests for information should be directed to: info@316publishing.com

ISBN: 978-1-63664-227-7

All scripture is from the New American Standard Bible. Copyright 1960, 1962, 1963, 1968, 1971, 1972, 1973, 1975, 1977, 1995 by the Lockman Foundation. The "NASB," "NAS," New American Standard Bible" and "New American Standard" trademarks are registered in the United States Patent and Trademark Office by the Lockman Foundation. Used by permission. For more information on permissions guidelines for the NASB, please visit Lockman.org.

All rights reserved.
No part of this publication may be reproduced, stored in a retrieval system, or transmitted in any form or by any means; electronic, photocopying, recording or otherwise without the prior written permission of the publisher.

Printed in China
29 28 27 26 25 24 23/3 4 5 6 7 8 9

EXPLANATION OF GENERAL FORMAT

Paragraphs are designated by bold face verse numbers or letters.

Personal Pronouns are capitalized when pertaining to Deity.

Brackets indicate words probably not in the original languages.

Italics are used in the text to indicate words which are not found in the original Hebrew, Aramaic, or Greek but implied by it.

Small caps in the New Testament are used in the text to indicate Old Testament quotations or obvious references to Old Testament texts. Variations of Old Testament wording are found in New Testament citations depending on whether the New Testament writer translated from a Hebrew text, used existing Greek or Aramaic translations, or paraphrased the material. It should be noted that modern rules for the indication of direct quotation were not used in biblical times; thus, the ancient writer would use exact quotations or references to quotation without specific indication of such.

An Asterisk (*) is used to mark verbs that are historical presents in the Greek which have been translated with an English past tense in order to conform to modern usage. The translators recognized that in some contexts the present tense seems more unexpected and unjustified to the English reader than a past tense would have been. But Greek authors frequently used the present tense for the sake of heightened vividness, thereby transporting their readers in imagination to the actual scene at the time of occurrence. However, the translators felt that it would be wise to change these historical presents to English past tenses.

EPHESIANS

1 Paul, an apostle of Christ Jesus by the will of God,
To the saints who are at Ephesus and *who are* faithful in Christ Jesus:

2 Grace to you and peace from God our Father and the Lord Jesus Christ.

3 Blessed *be* the God and Father of our Lord Jesus Christ, who has blessed us with every spiritual blessing in the heavenly *places* in Christ,

4 just as He chose us in Him before the foundation of the world, that we would be holy and blameless before Him. In love

5 He predestined us to adoption as sons through Jesus Christ to Himself, according to the kind intention of His will,

6 to the praise of the glory of His grace, which He freely bestowed on us in the Beloved.

7 In Him we have redemption through His blood, the forgiveness of our trespasses, according to the riches of His grace

8 which He lavished on us. In all wisdom and insight

9 He made known to us the mystery of His will, according to His kind intention which He purposed in Him

10 with a view to an administration suitable to the fullness of the times, *that is,* the summing up of all things in Christ, things in the heavens and things on the earth. In Him

11 also we have obtained an inheritance, having been predestined according to His purpose who works all things after the counsel of His will,

12 to the end that we who were the first to hope in Christ would be to the praise of His glory.

13 In Him, you also, after listening to the message of truth, the gospel of your salvation—having also believed, you were sealed in Him with the Holy Spirit of promise,

14 who is given as a pledge of our inheritance, with a view to the redemption of *God's own* possession, to the praise of His glory.

15 For this reason I too, having heard of the faith in the Lord Jesus which *exists* among you and your love for all the saints,

16 do not cease giving thanks for you, while making mention *of you* in my prayers;

17 that the God of our Lord Jesus Christ, the Father of glory, may give to you a spirit of wisdom and of revelation in the knowledge of Him.

18 *I pray that* the eyes of your heart may be enlightened, so that you will know what is the hope of His calling, what are the riches of the glory of His inheritance in the saints,

19 and what is the surpassing greatness of His power toward us who believe. *These are* in accordance with the working of the strength of His might

20 which He brought about in Christ, when He raised Him from the dead and seated Him at His right hand in the heavenly *places*,

21 far above all rule and authority and power and dominion, and every name that is named, not only in this age but also in the one to come.

22 And He put all things in subjection under His feet, and gave Him as head over all things to the church,

23 which is His body, the fullness of Him who fills all in all.

2 And you were dead in your trespasses and sins,

2 in which you formerly walked according to the course of this world, according to the prince of the power of the air, of the spirit that is now working in the sons of disobedience.

3 Among them we too all formerly lived in the lusts of our flesh, indulging the desires of the flesh and of the mind, and were by nature children of wrath, even as the rest.

4 But God, being rich in mercy, because of His great love with which He loved us,

5 even when we were dead in our transgressions, made us alive together with Christ (by grace you have been saved),

6 and raised us up with Him, and seated us with Him in the heavenly *places* in Christ Jesus,

7 so that in the ages to come He might show the surpassing riches of His grace in kindness toward us in Christ Jesus.

8 For by grace you have been saved through faith; and that not of yourselves, *it is* the gift of God;

9 not as a result of works, so that no one may boast.

10 For we are His workmanship, created in Christ Jesus for good works, which God prepared beforehand so that we would walk in them.

11 Therefore remember that formerly you, the Gentiles in the flesh, who are called "Uncircumcision" by the so-called "Circumcision," *which is* performed in the flesh by human hands—

12 *remember* that you were at that time separate from Christ, excluded from the commonwealth of Israel, and strangers to the covenants of promise, having no hope and without God in the world.

13 But now in Christ Jesus you who formerly were far off have been brought near by the blood of Christ.

14 For He Himself is our peace, who made both *groups into* one and broke down the barrier of the dividing wall,

15 by abolishing in His flesh the enmity, *which is* the Law of commandments *contained* in ordinances, so that in Himself He might make the two into one new man, *thus* establishing peace,

16 and might reconcile them both in one body to God through the cross, by it having put to death the enmity.

17 AND HE CAME AND PREACHED PEACE TO YOU WHO WERE FAR AWAY, AND PEACE TO THOSE WHO WERE NEAR;

18 for through Him we both have our access in one Spirit to the Father.

19 So then you are no longer strangers and aliens, but you are fellow citizens with the saints, and are of God's household,

20 having been built on the foundation of the apostles and prophets, Christ Jesus Himself being the corner *stone*,

21 in whom the whole building, being fitted together, is growing into a holy temple in the Lord,

22 in whom you also are being built together into a dwelling of God in the Spirit.

3 For this reason I, Paul, the prisoner of Christ Jesus for the sake of you Gentiles—

2 if indeed you have heard of the stewardship of God's grace which was given to me for you;

3 that by revelation there was made known to me the mystery, as I wrote before in brief.

4 By referring to this, when you read you can understand my insight into the mystery of Christ,

5 which in other generations was not made known to the sons of men, as it has now been revealed to His holy apostles and prophets in the Spirit;

6 *to be specific,* that the Gentiles are fellow heirs and fellow members of the body, and fellow partakers of the promise in Christ Jesus through the gospel,

7 of which I was made a minister, according to the gift of God's grace which was given to me according to the working of His power.

8 To me, the very least of all saints, this grace was given, to preach to the Gentiles the unfathomable riches of Christ,

9 and to bring to light what is the administration of the mystery which for ages has been hidden in God who created all things;

10 so that the manifold wisdom of God might now be made known through the church to the rulers and the authorities in the heavenly *places*.

11 *This was* in accordance with the eternal purpose which He carried out in Christ Jesus our Lord,

12 in whom we have boldness and confident access through faith in Him.

13 Therefore I ask you not to lose heart at my tribulations on your behalf, for they are your glory.

14 For this reason I bow my knees before the Father,

15 from whom every family in heaven and on earth derives its name,

16 that He would grant you, according to the riches of His glory, to be strengthened with power through His Spirit in the inner man,

17 so that Christ may dwell in your hearts through faith; *and* that you, being rooted and grounded in love,

18 may be able to comprehend with all the saints what is the breadth and length and height and depth,

19 and to know the love of Christ which surpasses knowledge, that you may be filled up to all the fullness of God.

20 Now to Him who is able to do far more abundantly beyond all that we ask or think, according to the power that works within us,

21 to Him *be* the glory in the church and in Christ Jesus to all generations forever and ever. Amen.

4 Therefore I, the prisoner of the Lord, implore you to walk in a manner worthy of the calling with which you have been called,

2 with all humility and gentleness, with patience, showing tolerance for one another in love,

3 being diligent to preserve the unity of the Spirit in the bond of peace.

4 *There is* one body and one Spirit, just as also you were called in one hope of your calling;

5 one Lord, one faith, one baptism,

6 one God and Father of all who is over all and through all and in all.

7 But to each one of us grace was given according to the measure of Christ's gift.

8 Therefore it says,
 "When He ascended on high,
 He led captive a host of captives,
 And He gave gifts to men."

9 (Now this *expression*, "He ascended," what does it mean except that He also had descended into the lower parts of the earth?

10 He who descended is Himself also He who ascended far above all the heavens, so that He might fill all things.)

11 And He gave some *as* apostles, and some *as* prophets, and some *as* evangelists, and some *as* pastors and teachers,

12 for the equipping of the saints for the work of service, to the building up of the body of Christ;

13 until we all attain to the unity of the faith, and of the knowledge of the Son of God, to a mature man, to the measure of the stature which belongs to the fullness of Christ.

14 As a result, we are no longer to be children, tossed here and there by waves and carried about by every wind of doctrine, by the trickery of men, by craftiness in deceitful scheming;

15 but speaking the truth in love, we are to grow up in all *aspects* into Him who is the head, *even* Christ,

16 from whom the whole body, being fitted and held together by what every joint supplies, according to the proper working of each individual part, causes the growth of the body for the building up of itself in love.

17 So this I say, and affirm together with the Lord, that you walk no longer just as the Gentiles also walk, in the futility of their mind,

18 being darkened in their understanding, excluded from the life of God because of the ignorance that is in them, because of the hardness of their heart;

19 and they, having become callous, have given themselves over to sensuality for the practice of every kind of impurity with greediness.

20 But you did not learn Christ in this way,

21 if indeed you have heard Him and have been taught in Him, just as truth is in Jesus,

22 that, in reference to your former manner of life, you lay aside the old self, which is being corrupted in accordance with the lusts of deceit,

23 and that you be renewed in the spirit of your mind,

24 and put on the new self, which in *the likeness of* God has been created in righteousness and holiness of the truth.

25 Therefore, laying aside falsehood, SPEAK TRUTH EACH ONE *of you* WITH HIS NEIGHBOR, for we are members of one another.

26 BE ANGRY, AND *yet* DO NOT SIN; do not let the sun go down on your anger,

27 and do not give the devil an opportunity.

28 He who steals must steal no longer; but rather he must labor, performing with his own hands what is good, so that he will have *something* to share with one who has need.

29 Let no unwholesome word proceed from your mouth, but only such *a word* as is good for edification according to the need *of the moment,* so that it will give grace to those who hear.

30 Do not grieve the Holy Spirit of God, by whom you were sealed for the day of redemption.

31 Let all bitterness and wrath and anger and clamor and slander be put away from you, along with all malice.

32 Be kind to one another, tender-hearted, forgiving each other, just as God in Christ also has forgiven you.

5

Therefore be imitators of God, as beloved children;

2 and walk in love, just as Christ also loved you and gave Himself up for us, an offering and a sacrifice to God as a fragrant aroma.

3 But immorality or any impurity or greed must not even be named among you, as is proper among saints;

4 and *there must be no* filthiness and silly talk, or coarse jesting, which are not fitting, but rather giving of thanks.

5 For this you know with certainty, that no immoral or impure person or covetous man, who is an idolater, has an inheritance in the kingdom of Christ and God.

6 Let no one deceive you with empty words, for because of these things the wrath of God comes upon the sons of disobedience.

7 Therefore do not be partakers with them;

8 for you were formerly darkness, but now you are Light in the Lord; walk as children of Light

9 (for the fruit of the Light *consists* in all goodness and righteousness and truth),

10 trying to learn what is pleasing to the Lord.

11 Do not participate in the unfruitful deeds of darkness, but instead even expose them;

12 for it is disgraceful even to speak of the things which are done by them in secret.

13 But all things become visible when they are exposed by the light, for everything that becomes visible is light.

14 For this reason it says,
   "Awake, sleeper,
   And arise from the dead,
   And Christ will shine on you."

15 Therefore be careful how you walk, not as unwise men but as wise,

16 making the most of your time, because the days are evil.

17 So then do not be foolish, but understand what the will of the Lord is.

18 And do not get drunk with wine, for that is dissipation, but be filled with the Spirit,

19 speaking to one another in psalms and hymns and spiritual songs, singing and making melody with your heart to the Lord;

20 always giving thanks for all things in the name of our Lord Jesus Christ to God, even the Father;

21 and be subject to one another in the fear of Christ.

22 Wives, *be subject* to your own husbands, as to the Lord.

23 For the husband is the head of the wife, as Christ also is the head of the church, He Himself *being* the Savior of the body.

24 But as the church is subject to Christ, so also the wives *ought to be* to their husbands in everything.

25 Husbands, love your wives, just as Christ also loved the church and gave Himself up for her,

26 so that He might sanctify her, having cleansed her by the washing of water with the word,

27 that He might present to Himself the church in all her glory, having no spot or wrinkle or any such thing; but that she would be holy and blameless.

28 So husbands ought also to love their own wives as their own bodies. He who loves his own wife loves himself;

29 for no one ever hated his own flesh, but nourishes and cherishes it, just as Christ also *does* the church,

30 because we are members of His body.

31 FOR THIS REASON A MAN SHALL LEAVE HIS FATHER AND MOTHER AND SHALL BE JOINED TO HIS WIFE, AND THE TWO SHALL BECOME ONE FLESH.

32 This mystery is great; but I am speaking with reference to Christ and the church.

33 Nevertheless, each individual among you also is to love his own wife even as himself, and the wife must *see to it* that she respects her husband.

6 Children, obey your parents in the Lord, for this is right.

2 HONOR YOUR FATHER AND MOTHER (which is the first commandment with a promise),

3 SO THAT IT MAY BE WELL WITH YOU, AND THAT YOU MAY LIVE LONG ON THE EARTH.

4 Fathers, do not provoke your children to anger, but bring them up in the discipline and instruction of the Lord.

5 Slaves, be obedient to those who are your masters according to the flesh, with fear and trembling, in the sincerity of your heart, as to Christ;

6 not by way of eyeservice, as men-pleasers, but as slaves of Christ, doing the will of God from the heart.

7 With good will render service, as to the Lord, and not to men,

8 knowing that whatever good thing each one does, this he will receive back from the Lord, whether slave or free.

9 And masters, do the same things to them, and give up threatening, knowing that both their Master and yours is in heaven, and there is no partiality with Him.

10 Finally, be strong in the Lord and in the strength of His might.

11 Put on the full armor of God, so that you will be able to stand firm against the schemes of the devil.

12 For our struggle is not against flesh and blood, but against the rulers, against the powers, against the world forces of this darkness, against the spiritual *forces* of wickedness in the heavenly *places.*

13 Therefore, take up the full armor of God, so that you will be able to resist in the evil day, and having done everything, to stand firm.

14 Stand firm therefore, HAVING GIRDED YOUR LOINS WITH TRUTH, and HAVING PUT ON THE BREASTPLATE OF RIGHTEOUSNESS,

15 and having shod YOUR FEET WITH THE PREPARATION OF THE GOSPEL OF PEACE;

16 in addition to all, taking up the shield of faith with which you will be able to extinguish all the flaming arrows of the evil *one.*

17 And take THE HELMET OF SALVATION, and the sword of the Spirit, which is the word of God.

18 With all prayer and petition pray at all times in the Spirit, and with this in view, be on the alert with all perseverance and petition for all the saints,

19 and *pray* on my behalf, that utterance may be given to me in the opening of my mouth, to make known with boldness the mystery of the gospel,

20 for which I am an ambassador in chains; that in *proclaiming* it I may speak boldly, as I ought to speak.

21 But that you also may know about my circumstances, how I am doing, Tychicus, the beloved brother and faithful minister in the Lord, will make everything known to you.

22 I have sent him to you for this very purpose, so that you may know about us, and that he may comfort your hearts.

23 Peace be to the brethren, and love with faith, from God the Father and the Lord Jesus Christ.

24 Grace be with all those who love our Lord Jesus Christ with incorruptible *love*.